POSTWAR AMERICA

THE COLD WAR

by Connor Stratton

ВПЕРЕД, К ПОБЕДЕ КОММУНИЗМА!

Б-2-88

FOCUS READERS.
NAVIGATOR

WWW.FOCUSREADERS.COM

Focus Readers is distributed by North Star Editions:
sales@northstareditions.com | 888-417-0195

Produced for Focus Readers by Red Line Editorial.

Content Consultant: Nicole Sackley, PhD, Associate Professor of History and American Studies, University of Richmond

Photographs ©: AP Images, cover, 1, 14, 22, 24–25; Bettmann/Getty Images, 4–5, 11, 12–13, 17; STR/AP Images, 7; Konrad Giehr/picture-alliance/dpa/AP Images, 8; Horst Faas/AP Images, 18–19; Department of Defense/AP Images, 20; Peter Turnley/Corbis Historical/VCG/Getty Images, 27; Red Line Editorial, 28

Library of Congress Cataloging-in-Publication Data
Names: Stratton, Connor, author.
Title: The Cold War / by Connor Stratton.
Description: Mendota Heights, MN : Focus Readers, [2024] | Series: Postwar America | Includes bibliographical references and index. | Audience: Grades 4-6
Identifiers: LCCN 2023027846 (print) | LCCN 2023027847 (ebook) | ISBN 9798889980407 (hardcover) | ISBN 9798889980834 (paperback) | ISBN 9798889981640 (pdf) | ISBN 9798889981268 (ebook)
Subjects: LCSH: Cold War--Juvenile literature.
Classification: LCC D843 .S8384 2024 (print) | LCC D843 (ebook) | DDC 909.82/5--dc23/eng/20230613
LC record available at https://lccn.loc.gov/2023027846
LC ebook record available at https://lccn.loc.gov/2023027847

Printed in the United States of America
Mankato, MN
012024

ABOUT THE AUTHOR
Connor Stratton writes and edits nonfiction children's books. He lives in Minnesota.

TABLE OF CONTENTS

CHAPTER 1

FROM WORLD WAR TO COLD WAR

World War II (1939–1945) caused massive destruction. The war weakened many European countries. Japan was weak, too. These countries were losing their **colonies**. However, the United States was in a stronger military position. So was the Soviet Union. These two countries were called superpowers.

Approximately 60 million people died during World War II. Most victims were civilians.

The United States and the Soviet Union had been **allies** during the war. But they were very different. The United States had a capitalist economy. In this system, individuals own property. They control how goods are made. The United States also had a democratic government. People chose their leaders in elections.

The Soviet Union had a Communist economy. Communism calls for all property to be owned by the public. The Soviet government decided how goods were made. Also, one **party** held control. People did not choose their leaders.

Both superpowers wanted to spread their systems around the world. As a

Soviet citizens who spoke out against the government were sent to prison camps. They were forced to work.

result, they stopped being allies. Each tried to limit the other's power.

In 1947, US leaders put forward a plan. They wanted to stop Communism from spreading. In 1948, the United States started giving money to countries in Western Europe. That way, the countries could rebuild.

The countries that won World War II split Germany in half. Germany remained divided for 45 years.

The Soviet Union responded. It began aid programs for countries in Eastern Europe. As a result, Europe became sharply divided. This divide kept Germany split in half. The United States influenced West Germany. The Soviet Union influenced East Germany.

The United States and the Soviet Union never fought each other directly. That's why the conflict became known as the Cold War. Instead, the two superpowers competed in other ways. They formed alliances with other countries. They also built many nuclear weapons.

FORMING ALLIANCES

The North Atlantic Treaty Organization (NATO) was formed in 1949. This group of countries agreed to defend one another. Members included the United States, Canada, and much of Western Europe. The Soviet Union wanted to counter NATO. So, it created the Warsaw Pact in 1955. This group included much of Eastern Europe.

NUCLEAR TESTING

During the Cold War, the United States and the Soviet Union tested thousands of nuclear weapons. These tests often took place in the Pacific Ocean.

When Nerje Joseph was young, her family lived on Rongelap. This area is part of the Marshall Islands. "We worked together, we ate together, we played together," Joseph said.[1] That changed on March 1, 1954. The United States performed a nuclear test. It happened miles away from Rongelap. But a few hours later, **radioactive** powder fell. It landed on Joseph and others. They soon became sick. Their skin was burned, and their hair fell out.

Joseph and her family had to move away from Rongelap. But their problems remained. When

Nuclear weapons are powerful enough to destroy entire cities.

Joseph grew up, she got cancer. This disease is common for people who are near nuclear tests.

"I can go back, but I don't know," Joseph said in 2020. "They told me it is still nuclear active."[2] Two years later, Joseph died at age 74. She was never able to return home.

1. Susanne Rust. "How the U.S. betrayed the Marshall Islands, kindling the next nuclear disaster." *Los Angeles Times*. Los Angeles Times, 19 Nov. 2019. Web. 11 Apr. 2023.
2. Sam Denby, director. *The Final Years of Majuro*. Wendover Productions, 2020. 1 hr., 5 min.

CHAPTER 2

PROXY WARS

The Cold War involved several **proxy wars**. One example was the Korean War (1950–1953). This conflict was between North Korea and South Korea. North Korea received support from the Soviet Union. It also got help from China, another Communist country. The United States and its allies fought with South

Nearly three million people died in the Korean War. Many others lost their homes.

 With the help of the United States, Iran's army removed the country's democratically elected leader.

Korea's army. Neither side won. Korea remained divided.

US and Soviet leaders forced their influence all over the world. In 1953, the United States worked with the United Kingdom to overthrow Iran's leader. They made sure the new leader would be their ally. The next year, the United States overthrew Guatemala's leader. Then, in 1956, Soviet forces invaded Hungary. They stopped a group that was trying to end Communism in Hungary.

A THIRD WAY?

After World War II, dozens of countries gained **independence** from their colonizers. Many countries didn't want to choose sides in the Cold War. They did not want either superpower to control them. Instead, they wanted to go their own way. India and Indonesia led this path in Asia. Yugoslavia led in Europe. Egypt, Ghana, and Algeria led in Africa. These countries worked together. But US and Soviet actions forced them into the Cold War.

Congo gained independence in 1960. The Central African country became free from Belgium. But one area still supported Belgium. It split off from Congo. Belgium sent troops to support it. US leaders sided with Belgium. They threatened Congo's leader, Patrice Lumumba. And in 1961, Belgian-led forces killed Lumumba. A proxy war continued in the country for several years.

In 1961, the United States tried to overthrow the Communist leader of Cuba. The plan failed. After that, Cuba became allies with the Soviet Union. The Soviet Union also pledged to protect Cuba. In 1962, the Soviet Union began sending

A Soviet ship carries nuclear weapons away from Cuba in 1962.

nuclear weapons there. However, a US spy plane discovered them. Nuclear war almost took place. US and Soviet leaders talked with each other. Finally, the Soviet Union removed the weapons. The event was called the Cuban Missile Crisis.

CHAPTER 3

VIETNAM AND DÉTENTE

By the 1960s, the Vietnam War (1954–1975) had been going on for several years. Some Vietnamese people wanted a capitalist country. Others wanted Vietnam to be Communist. Cold War powers joined the fighting. The United States sent troops to support South Vietnam. Meanwhile, the Soviet

The Vietnam War resulted in millions of deaths and massive destruction to the country.

Millions of people fled Vietnam after the war. Many died at sea.

Union and China supported North Vietnam.

Communist forces won the war. They united the country. However, millions of Vietnamese people had been killed. Tens of thousands of US soldiers also died. The war also destroyed much of Vietnam. Laos and Cambodia were harmed, too.

By the 1970s, the Soviet Union and China were no longer allies. This split weakened the Communist world. Meanwhile, Japan and Western Europe had rebounded from World War II. They were stronger than ever before.

The United States was still competing with the Soviet Union. But leaders had learned from the past. They wanted to avoid another Cuban Missile Crisis. They wanted to avoid another Vietnam War, too. US leaders did not want those kinds of costs and risks.

 In 1972, Chinese leader Mao Zedong (left) met with US president Richard Nixon.

As a result, the Cold War became less extreme. This shift was called détente. It means "relaxation" in French. Nuclear war became less likely. The United States also began friendlier relations with China.

However, fighting still happened. For example, Angola gained independence in 1975. A civil war broke out. Soviet and Cuban forces supported one side. The United States supported the other.

WINNING AT ALL COSTS

The United States and the Soviet Union both wanted the world to follow their way of doing things. But as the Cold War went on, both sides started to care more about defeating the other. To achieve that goal, both countries wanted allies they could control. As a result, both sides tried to change other countries' governments. For example, the United States helped remove several democratically elected leaders around the world. The new leaders did not believe in democracy. But they were easier to control.

CHAPTER 4

END OF THE COLD WAR

The period of détente ended in 1979. That year, the Soviet Union invaded Afghanistan. Soviet troops fought to support Communist forces there. In response, the United States helped the other side. It was another proxy war.

Latin American countries also became caught in the Cold War's conflict. For

Afghan fighters pose near a captured Soviet tank in 1980.

instance, a **socialist** group gained power in Nicaragua in 1979. Armed fighters worked to overthrow the group. The United States backed them. Cuba and the Soviet Union supported the other side.

US leaders also supported several military leaders. In Central America, this included the leaders of Guatemala and El Salvador. The United States also backed brutal governments across South America. These governments stopped many groups that were pushing for change. The groups did not threaten the United States. But US leaders wanted to make sure systems similar to Communism did not take hold.

Violence in Central America forced millions of people to leave their homes. Many people fled to the United States.

Meanwhile, the war in Afghanistan continued throughout the 1980s. However, the Soviet economy was struggling. Soviet leaders wanted to rebuild at home. That meant ending the war in Afghanistan.

The Cold War was nearing its end. Soviet forces left Afghanistan in 1989.

That same year, many Eastern European countries overthrew their Communist governments. In 1990, Germany was reunited as one country. And in 1991, the

MAJOR CONFLICTS OF THE COLD WAR

The United States and the Soviet Union did not fight each other directly. However, their actions caused many conflicts around the globe.

Soviet Union fell apart. It split into 15 countries. They stretched across Eastern Europe and Central Asia. The largest was Russia. These countries held elections. They also shifted to capitalist economies.

The Cold War was finally over. The United States was the world's only superpower. It continued to dominate for years to come.

COLD WAR LEGACIES

The Cold War left devastation around the world. Millions of people died in proxy wars. Entire regions became unstable. And some countries were cut off from much of the world. North Korea and Cuba were two examples. Their leaders were **authoritarian**. People there suffered as a result.

FOCUS ON
THE COLD WAR

Write your answers on a separate piece of paper.

1. Write a paragraph explaining the main ideas of Chapter 1.

2. Do you think countries should have nuclear weapons? Why or why not?

3. When did the Cuban Missile Crisis take place?
   - **A.** 1950
   - **B.** 1962
   - **C.** 1989

4. Why might nuclear weapons have caused the United States and the Soviet Union to avoid a direct war with each other?
   - **A.** Leaders didn't know how the weapons would work.
   - **B.** Only one side of the conflict had nuclear weapons.
   - **C.** Nuclear weapons could destroy much of the world.

Answer key on page 32.

GLOSSARY

allies
Nations or people that are on the same side during a war.

authoritarian
Putting the power of the government above the freedoms of the people.

colonies
Areas taken over and controlled by another country.

independence
The ability to make decisions without being controlled by another government.

party
A group that has specific ideas about how the government should be run.

proxy wars
Wars in which powerful countries support opposite sides in conflicts between weaker countries.

radioactive
Giving off dangerous energy.

socialist
Supporting a political system in which the government provides for basic needs, and where workers control the economy.

TO LEARN MORE

BOOKS

Gitlin, Marty. *Postwar America*. Ann Arbor, MI: Cherry Lake Publishing, 2022.

Hamilton, John. *Missiles and Spy Satellites*. Minneapolis: Abdo Publishing, 2019.

Herschbach, Elisabeth. *Aftermath of World War II*. Mendota Heights, MN: Focus Readers, 2023.

NOTE TO EDUCATORS

Visit **www.focusreaders.com** to find lesson plans, activities, links, and other resources related to this title.

INDEX

Answer Key: 1. Answers will vary; 2. Answers will vary; 3. B; 4. C